THE
KEY WEST
BUCKET LIST

100 WAYS TO HAVE A REAL
FLORIDA KEYS EXPERIENCE

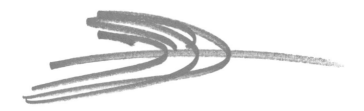

DAVID L. SLOAN

PHANTOM**PRESS**
K E Y W E S T

legal disclaimer

This book is designed to provide information, entertainment, and motivation to our readers. It is sold with the understanding that the publisher is not engaged to render any type of physical, psychological, legal, or any other kind of professional advice.

Participation in the activities listed may be dangerous or illegal and could lead to arrest, serious injury, or death.

The content of this book is the sole expression and opinion of its author and not necessarily that of the publisher. No warranties or guarantees are expressed or implied.

Neither the publisher nor the individual author shall be liable for any physical, psychological, emotional, financial, or commercial damages, including, but not limited to, special, incidental, consequential, or other damages.

Our views and rights are the same: you are responsible for your own choices, actions, and results.

dedication

To the people who instilled purpose and inspire my adventurous nature: my parents, Tod and Eileen Sloan, my sister, Kristen whatever-last-name-you-are-going-by-now, and the Confucius Cowboy, Rob Marjerison. Thank you.

acknowledgements

This book would not exist without the following people (and several more whose names slip my mind as I have been drinking).

Motivation: Christopher Shultz
Editing, Layout, Design: Marc Phelps
Cover Design: Michael Marrero
Photography: Rob O'Neal, Michael Marrero, Nick Doll
Research & Editing: Rachel Curran
Editing: Laura Theobald
Concept Development: Larry Bradley, Charles Belanger, Mandy Miles, Stan Miles, Elizabeth Love, Gregg McGrady, John Nolte, Shane Liddick, Terry Schmida, Kim Sklar, Alan Nelson, Carol Shaughnessy, Mary DeSilva, Tricia Palmer, Robert Ban, Liz Miller, William Ellis, Michael Crisp, Brett Southgate, Stephanie Hughes, Kelly Martin Kersey, Oliver Belanger, Frank Holden, Jean Thornton, Melissa Clarke, Tim Schwarz, and the most important person of them all, _____ (your name here).

THE
KEY WEST
BUCKET LIST

100 WAYS TO HAVE A REAL
FLORIDA KEYS EXPERIENCE

DAVID L. SLOAN

why a bucket list?

The original title for this book was *100 Things To Do in Key West & the Florida Keys Before You Die*. It started several years ago when I overheard an all-too-common conversation taking place between two couples, brought together by the simple fact that they both needed refills of their Rum Runners at the same time.

"What have you done in Key West?" the lady from Pennsylvania asked. The Minnesota couple rattled off a typical response.

"We rode the Conch Train, did the Hemingway House, went snorkeling, walked down Duval Street ..."

When the question was asked reciprocally, the Pennsylvania couple had a similar response.

Both couples probably planned their vacations for some time. They had most likely spent a good amount of money on travel, lodging, and entertainment. All of them seemed to be having a good time, but something was missing: all four were visiting the Keys, yet not a one was "experiencing" the Keys. They were missing out, but it wasn't their fault.

We live an in age of informational bombardment. Key West, like every tourist town, has so much to see and do in so little time. It's easy to become so focused on the destination that we lose site of the journey, but it is in the journey that we overcome obstacles, step out of our comfort zones, forge new relationships, and experience the magic. As sappy as it sounds, I've experienced that magic firsthand, and I think I can share it, or at least send you down that magical path with the content in the following pages.

what to expect

1. No Instruction Manual:

I've never been a fan of the instructional guidebook that tells you what to do and how to do it with tips for the best results. I know what I like. Tell me something worth doing, and I'll tailor it to my desires. That's the approach I'm taking here. Once you get a few check marks under your belt, you will understand why.

2. Adventure & Challenge:

Consider the list a primer for adventure. Some tasks are easy to accomplish, some are difficult, and some are close to impossible. The mix is intended to introduce you to new experiences in unique locations that define the Florida Keys. Take things at your own pace. No one is grading your performance.

3. Inspiration:

I like to think I know it all, but a fresh perspective has never done me wrong. I'm not qualified to dish out any words of wisdom that leave you feeling warm and tingly with a sense of purpose, so I called in the experts. Mark Twain, Helen Keller, Eleanor Roosevelt, and Rudyard Kipling are all contributors with quotes that lend a deeper meaning to each adventure.

4. Satisfaction:

Whether you fill the list at the end with fat red check marks and seek out every adventure from 1-100 or just take the journeys in your mind from the comfort of your favorite chair, this book should leave you with a sense of satisfaction. If it doesn't, let me know. Life is about evolving and a little constructive criticism can go a long way. Feeling supercharged? Want to share your adventures with others? There's a place for that, too. Visit www.FatRedPen.com to share your thoughts, experiences, photos, and new additions to the list.

So why the change in title? *100 Things To Do Before You Die* had too much of an emphasis on dying. This is a book about living.

Enjoy.
David L. Sloan

" There are two kinds of adventurers: those who go truly hoping to find adventure and those who go secretly hoping they won't. "

— **Rabindranath Tagore**

1

close the
green parrot

"I should never have switched from Scotch to martinis."

— Humphrey Bogart's last words

2

hand-feed
a tarpon

"Many men go fishing all of their lives without knowing it is not fish they are after."

— Henry David Thoreau

3

wear nothing
but body paint

"We are all sculptors and painters, and our material is our own flesh, and blood, and bones."

— **Henry David Thoreau**

4

stay in a
haunted hotel

"You gain strength, courage, and confidence by every experience by which you really stop to look fear in the face. You are able to say to yourself, 'I lived through this horror. I can take the next thing that comes along.'"

— Eleanor Roosevelt

5

ride a bike
in the rain

"Remember, even though the outside world might be raining, if you keep on smiling, the sun will soon show its face and smile back at you."

—*Anna Lee*

6

catch your
own lobster

*" Searching is half the fun: life is much
more manageable when thought of as a
scavenger hunt as opposed to a surprise party. "*

— *Jimmy Buffett*

7

skinny dip
in the ocean

"Only when the tide goes out do you discover who's been swimming naked."

— **Warren Buffett**

8

find the perfect
picnic spot

As is the gardener, so is the garden.

— **Proverb**

9

cut through
the cemetery
at midnight

" The cemeteries are filled with people who thought the world couldn't get along without them. "

—American Proverb

10

play with a
hemingway cat

*" A cat has absolute emotional honesty: human beings,
for one reason or another, may hide their feelings, but a
cat does not. "*

— Ernest Hemingway

11

hit the
dance floor
at sloppy joe's

"To dance is to be out of yourself. Larger, more beautiful, more powerful. This is power; it is glory on earth and it is yours for the taking."

—Agnes de Mille

12

light a candle in the hurricane grotto

"Thousands of candles can be lit from a single candle, and the life of the candle will not be shortened. Happiness never decreases by being shared."

— Buddha

13

taste fresh conch salad after you watch it being prepared

" *People ask me: 'Why do you write about food, and eating, and drinking? Why don't you write about the struggle for power and security, and about love, the way the others do?' The easiest answer is to say that, like most other humans, I am hungry.* "

— *M.F.K. Fisher*

14

attend a
gospel mass
and sing

"A bird doesn't sing because it has an answer, it sings because it has a song."

— *Maya Angelou*

15

see the island by air ... in a stunt plane

"I watch out my window as the planes take off into space. Oh, that I could fly away and start fresh. But I must realize that fresh starts also come in the pretty wrapped gift called 'tomorrow.'"

— **Unknown**

16

order a cheeseburger in paradise and land shark lager at margaritaville

"I love that whole princess mentality, but I also like throwing my hair in a ponytail, and just wearing jeans, going on a hike, and then eating a big chili-cheeseburger."

— Jennifer Love Hewitt

17

camp at
fort jefferson

"By its very nature the beautiful is isolated from everything else. From beauty no road leads to reality."

— **Hannah Arendt**

18

take in a sunset without the crowd

One of the greatest necessities in America is to discover creative solitude.

— *Carl Sandburg*

19

stay up and watch the sunrise on new year's day

" If every year is a marble, how many marbles do you have left? How many sunrises, how many opportunities to rise to the full stature of your being? "

— Joy Page

20

visit the prison petting zoo

" All (zoos) actually offer to the public in return for the taxes spent upon them is a form of idle and witless amusement, compared to which a visit to a penitentiary ... is informing, stimulating, and ennobling "

— Henry Louis Mencken

21

stand under the a.c. of a duval street shop on a hot summer day

"Oh, my God, this amazing cool breeze is coming through my window and the sun is shining. I'm happy."

— *Liv Tyler*

22

admire the city from a rooftop on a windy night

"It is easier to go down a hill than up, but the view is best from the top."

—Andrew Bennett

23

watch for
shooting stars from
the bat tower

" I see myself as a huge fiery comet, a shooting star.
Everyone stops, points up, and gasps, 'Oh, look at that!' Then,
whoosh, and I'm gone ... and they'll never see anything like it
ever again ... and they won't be able to forget me — ever. "

— Jim Morrison

24

watch the
shrimp boats
unload a
fresh catch

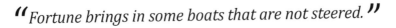

"Fortune brings in some boats that are not steered."

— William Shakespeare

25

jump from the sugarloaf bridge

"Sometimes, if you aren't sure about something, you just have to jump off the bridge and grow your wings on the way down."

— **Danielle Steel**

26

dig through
historic photos
at the library

"In twenty years you'll look back at photos of yourself and recall in a way you can't grasp now how much possibility lay before you and how fabulous you really looked."

— **Mary Schmich**

27

learn to blow
a conch shell

"You are the music while the music lasts."

— *T.S. Eliot*

28

climb to the top of the lighthouse

"Inside my empty bottle I was constructing a lighthouse while all the others were making ships."

— **Charles Simic**

29

pick a coconut, crack it, and drink the milk

"There is sweet water inside a tender coconut. Who poured the water inside the coconut? Was it the work of any man? No. Only the Divine can do such a thing."

— **Sri Sathya Sai Baba**

30

climb a
banyan tree

"One that would have the fruit must climb the tree."

— Thomas Fuller

31

spot a celebrity

"A celebrity is a person who works hard all his life to become well-known, then wears dark glasses to avoid being recognized."

— *Fred Allen*

32

jog, walk, or bike the 7-mile bridge

"I see my path, but I don't know where it leads. Not knowing where I'm going is what inspires me to travel it."

— **Rosalia de Castro**

33

build a
sand castle
on your legs

"*Sand castle virtues are all swept away, in the tidal destruction, the moral melee.*"

— *Jethro Tull*

34

drive the overseas highway in a convertible

" Twenty years from now you will be more disappointed by the things that you didn't do than by the ones you did do. So throw off the bowlines. Sail away from the safe harbor. Catch the trade winds in your sails. Explore. Dream. Discover. "

— ***Mark Twain***

35

spot a key deer

"They run like deer, jump like deer, and think like deer."

— *Charles Barkley*

36

get your quarter
in the lucky
fish and
make a wish

*"Life is like a coin. You can spend it any way you wish, but
you only spend it once."*

— **Lillian Dickson**

37

drink with a drag queen

"*I do not think of you as a man, and I do not think of you as a woman ... I think of you as an angel.*"

— *Stockard Channing*
as Carol Ann in "To Wong Foo"

38

meet enough people to earn a nickname

39

sip a real
cuban coffee

"*If I asked for a cup of coffee, someone would search for the double meaning.*"

— *Mae West*

40

create a
work of art

41

do something unique at the southernmost point

"I work everywhere, but I work best here."

— Tennessee Williams

42

dive a
shipwreck

" *Today is the day.* "

— *Mel Fisher*

43

make a key lime pie

"Have it jest as you've a mind to, but I've proved it time on time, If you want to change her nature, you have got to give her lime."

— **Rudyard Kipling**

44

wear a costume when no one else does

" *If the cut of the costume indicates intellect and talent, then the color indicates temper and heart.* "

— *Thomas Carlyle*

45

call the *citizen*'s voice with an entertaining comment

"Most of our misfortunes are more supportable than the comments of our friends upon them."

— **Charles Caleb Colton**

46

party with the mayor

47

learn to spearfish

" The charm of fishing is that it is the pursuit of that which is elusive but attainable, a perpetual series of occasions for hope. "

—Author Unknown

48

get naked in public without being arrested

"*I think on-stage nudity is disgusting, shameful, and damaging to all things American. But if I were 22 with a great body, it would be artistic, tasteful, patriotic, and a progressive religious experience.*"

— **Shelley Winters**

49

ride out
a hurricane

"If we must lose wife or husband when we live to our highest right, we lose an unhappy marriage as well, and we gain ourselves. But if a marriage is born between two already self-discovered, what a lovely adventure begins, hurricanes and all."

— Richard Bach

50

ride a
parade float

" When the parade began, Lloyd came out of the bookstore and was standing on the sidewalk. And when he saw me he called out in a very loud voice: 'JOE! Isn't this wonderful! Isn't this a marvelous day! Can you imagine this ever happening?' "

— **Joseph Hansen**

51

find a secret parking spot

" In some ... neighborhoods, looking for a parking space is not unlike panning for gold. "

— Gary Washburn

52

spot a bald eagle

"The eagle may soar; beavers build dams."

—**Joseph S. Nye, Jr.**

53

watch a
sea turtle hatch

"*Looking for peace is like looking for a turtle with a mustache: you won't be able to find it. But when your heart is ready, peace will come looking for you.*"

—**Ajahn Chah**

54

see a green flash

> *What is life? It is the flash of a firefly in the night. It is the breath of a buffalo in the wintertime. It is the little shadow which runs across the grass and loses itself in the sunset.*
>
> — **Crowfoot**

55

hoist the sail on
a schooner

" Wisdom sails with wind and time. "

— *John Florio*

56

dress like
a pirate

"Why join the navy if you can be a pirate?"

— **Steve Jobs**

57

attend a meeting
of the key west
breakfast club

*"It reminded him of his Uncle Seamus, the notorious and
poetic drunk, who would sit down at the breakfast table the
morning after a bender, drain a bottle of stout, and say, 'Ah,
the chill of consciousness returns.'"*

— *Molly O'Neill*

58

wave to a group of sightseeing tourists

"Since you cannot do good to all, you are to pay special attention to those who, by the accidents of time, or place, or circumstances, are brought into closer connection with you."

—Augustine of Hippo

59

snorkel with sharks

"Believe me! The secret of reaping the greatest fruitfulness and the greatest enjoyment from life is to live dangerously!"

— **Friedrich Nietzsche**

60

search for flamingos from a kayak

"Is there anything more beautiful than a beautiful, beautiful flamingo, flying across in front of a beautiful sunset? And he's carrying a beautiful rose in his beak, and also he's carrying a very beautiful painting with his feet. And also, you're drunk."

—*Jack Handy*

61

spend the night on a houseboat

"Fortune brings in some boats that are not steered."

— **William Shakespeare**

62

watch a meteor shower from sea

" I would rather be a superb meteor, every atom of me in magnificent glow, than a sleepy and permanent planet. "

—*Jack London*

63

dispose of a piece of trash that isn't yours

"There aren't many things that are universally cool, and it's cool not to litter. I'd never do it."

— Matthew McConaughey

64

complete the duval crawl

"An intelligent man is sometimes forced to be drunk to spend time with his fools."

— Ernest Hemingway

65

watch the conch shell drop on new year's eve

"We will open the book. Its pages are blank. We are going to put words on them ourselves. The book is called 'Opportunity' and its first chapter is New Year's Day."

— Edith Lovejoy Pierce

66

pick an avocado, make fresh guacamole, and plant the seed

"A tree is known by its fruit; a man by his deeds. A good deed is never lost; he who sows courtesy reaps friendship, and he who plants kindness gathers love."

— **St. Basil**

67

ascend to the top of mount trashmore

> "The way to Heaven is ascending; we must be content to travel uphill, though it be hard, and tiresome, and contrary to the natural bias of our flesh."
>
> —*Jonathan Edwards*

68

leave your dollar at the no name pub

" Without question, the greatest invention in the history of mankind is beer. Oh, I grant you that the wheel was also a fine invention, but the wheel does not go nearly as well with pizza. "

— **Dave Barry**

69

find an animal at the blue hole

"Don't taunt the alligator until after you've crossed the creek."

— *Dan Rather*

70

snorkel christ
of the abyss

"If I take the wings of the morning and swell in the uttermost parts of the sea, even there your hand will lead me and your right hand hold me fast."

— Psalm 139

71

make a list of things you love about the keys

"One of the secrets of getting more done is to make a To-Do List every day, keep it visible, and use it as a guide to action as you go through the day."

—Jean de La Fontaine

72

leave a message
in a bottle

"Life is like a message in a bottle, to be carried by the winds and the tides."

— **Gene Tierney**

73

join in the
conch republic's
bloody battle

*"A man should never put on his best trousers when he goes
out to battle for freedom and truth. "*

— **Henrik Ibsen**

74

lift a gold bar

"Silver and gold are not the only coin; virtue too passes current all over the world."

— Euripides

75

find the best cuban mix on the island

"*The small businessman is smart; he realizes there's no free lunch. On the other hand, he knows where to go to get a good inexpensive sandwich.*"

—*Adam Osborne*

76

sneak into a hotel hot tub

"They (the hot tubs) are warming up right now and by the time of the jump they should be steaming and lovely."

— **Connie Hagler**

77

visit the statues
of five oversized
sea creatures

"Objects which are usually the motives of our travels by land and by sea are often overlooked and neglected if they lie under our eye. We put off from time to time going and seeing what we know we have an opportunity of seeing when we please."

— *Plutarch*

78

buy a plant from the marc house

"See how nature — trees, flowers, grass — grows in silence ...We need silence to be able to touch souls."

— **Mother Teresa**

79

search for sea glass

"The sea does not reward those who are too anxious, too greedy, or too impatient. One should lie empty, open, choiceless as a beach — waiting for a gift from the sea."

—Anne Morrow Lindbergh

80

watch the bats come out at dusk

"Suspicions amongst thoughts are like bats amongst birds; they ever fly by twilight."

— **Francis Bacon**

81

find the
cashmier goats

"*Don't approach a goat from the front, a horse from the
back, or a fool from any side.*"

— *Yiddish Proverb*

82

nap in a
hammock

"A nap, my friend, is a brief period of sleep which overtakes
superannuated persons when they endeavor to entertain
unwelcome visitors or to listen to scientific lectures."

— *George Bernard Shaw*

83

befriend and name a
key west chicken

*"We can see a thousand miracles around us every day.
What is more supernatural than an egg yolk
turning into a chicken?"*

— S. Parkes Cadman

84

learn to identify key west's architectural styles

" ... I was increasingly attracted to and struck by [the] beautiful design of the eyebrow houses, with their front porch roofs extending demurely over the second-story windows ... which are unique to Key West and not found anywhere else in the country. "

—Alex Caemmerer,
from "The Houses of Key West"

85

visit robert the doll ... if you dare

> *"Be careful of the things you possess or they may end up possessing you."*
>
> — ***David Sloan***

86

spend a day
doing nothing

" Doing nothing is better than being busy doing nothing. "

— **Lao Tzu**

87

nurse a hangover
in the sunshine

*"Always do sober what you said you'd do drunk. That will
teach you to keep your mouth shut. "*

— **Ernest Hemingway**

88

get a tattoo

"Good tattoos aren't cheap, and cheap tattoos aren't good."

—Author Unknown

89

wear a t-shirt with a silly saying around town

"Do, every day, something no one else would be silly enough to do. It is bad for the mind to continually be part of unanimity."

— **Christopher Morley**

90

push your taste buds to the limit with a hot sauce tasting

" Love is like a friendship caught on fire. In the beginning, a flame, very pretty, often hot and fierce, but still only light and flickering. As love grows older, our hearts mature and our love becomes as coals; deep-burning and unquenchable. "

— ***Bruce Lee***

91

snap your photo
at mile marker zero

"It's never crowded along the extra mile."

— **Wayne Dyer**

92

talk with a homeless person and learn their story

"Be your own self with all people whether they be king or homeless."

— William Danforth

93

invent your own tropical drink

" Who was the first guy that looked at a cow and said, 'I think that I'll drink whatever comes out of those things when I squeeze them?' "

— ***Calvin & Hobbes***

94

volunteer at a charity event

"*Where there is charity and wisdom, there is neither fear nor ignorance.*"

— *St. Francis of Assisi*

95

spot a
water spout

" Iron rusts from disuse; water loses its purity from stagnation. ... Even so does inaction sap the vigour of the mind. "

— **Leonardo da Vinci**

96

dangle your legs
off the old
bahia honda bridge

*"We can't cross that bridge until we come to it, but I always
like to lay down a pontoon ahead of time."*

— **Bernard Baruch**

97

win a game of 801 bingo

"It's not true that nice guys finish last. Nice guys are winners before the game even starts."

—**Addison Walker**

98

explore a side road in the middle keys

" *Two roads diverged in a wood, and I — I took the one less traveled by, and that has made all the difference.* "

— ***Robert Frost***

99

enter the hemingway
look-alike contest,
no matter who
you look like

*"The real contest is always between what you've done and
what you're capable of doing. You measure yourself against
yourself and nobody else. "*

— **Geoffrey Gaberino**

100

have a drink with the author of this book

"Some writers take to drink, others take to audiences."

— **Gore Vidal**

i did it

Check off your accomplishments with a fat red pen!

- ☐ 1. close the green parrot
- ☐ 2. hand-feed a tarpon
- ☐ 3. wear nothing but body paint
- ☐ 4. stay in a haunted hotel
- ☐ 5. ride a bike in the rain
- ☐ 6. catch your own lobster
- ☐ 7. skinny dip in the ocean
- ☐ 8. find the perfect picnic spot
- ☐ 9. cut through the cemetery at midnight
- ☐ 10. play with a hemingway cat
- ☐ 11. hit the dance floor at sloppy joe's
- ☐ 12. light a candle in the hurricane grotto
- ☐ 13. taste fresh conch salad after you watch it being prepared
- ☐ 14. attend a gospel mass and sing
- ☐ 15. see the island by air... in a stunt plane
- ☐ 16. order a cheeseburger in paradise and land shark lager at margaritaville
- ☐ 17. camp at fort jefferson
- ☐ 18. take in a sunset without the crowd
- ☐ 19. stay up to watch the sunrise on new year's day

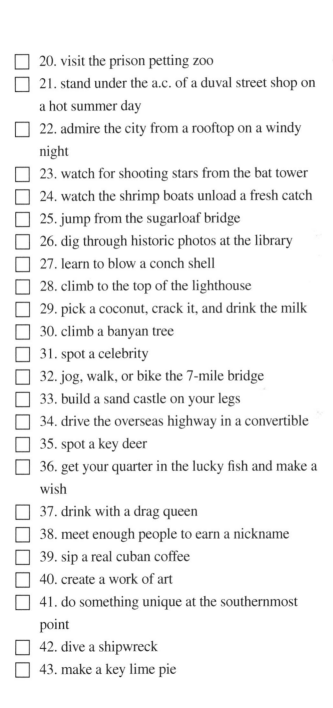

- [ ] 20. visit the prison petting zoo
- [ ] 21. stand under the a.c. of a duval street shop on a hot summer day
- [ ] 22. admire the city from a rooftop on a windy night
- [ ] 23. watch for shooting stars from the bat tower
- [ ] 24. watch the shrimp boats unload a fresh catch
- [ ] 25. jump from the sugarloaf bridge
- [ ] 26. dig through historic photos at the library
- [ ] 27. learn to blow a conch shell
- [ ] 28. climb to the top of the lighthouse
- [ ] 29. pick a coconut, crack it, and drink the milk
- [ ] 30. climb a banyan tree
- [ ] 31. spot a celebrity
- [ ] 32. jog, walk, or bike the 7-mile bridge
- [ ] 33. build a sand castle on your legs
- [ ] 34. drive the overseas highway in a convertible
- [ ] 35. spot a key deer
- [ ] 36. get your quarter in the lucky fish and make a wish
- [ ] 37. drink with a drag queen
- [ ] 38. meet enough people to earn a nickname
- [ ] 39. sip a real cuban coffee
- [ ] 40. create a work of art
- [ ] 41. do something unique at the southernmost point
- [ ] 42. dive a shipwreck
- [ ] 43. make a key lime pie

- [ ] 44. wear a costume when no one else does
- [ ] 45. call the *citizen*'s voice with an entertaining comment
- [ ] 46. party with the mayor
- [ ] 47. learn to spearfish
- [ ] 48. get naked in public without being arrested
- [ ] 49. ride out a hurricane
- [ ] 50. ride a parade float
- [ ] 51. find a secret parking spot
- [ ] 52. spot a bald eagle
- [ ] 53. watch a sea turtle hatch
- [ ] 54. see a green flash
- [ ] 55. hoist the sail on a schooner
- [ ] 56. dress like a pirate
- [ ] 57. attend a meeting of the key west breakfast club
- [ ] 58. wave to a group of sightseeing tourists
- [ ] 59. snorkel with sharks
- [ ] 60. search for flamingos from a kayak
- [ ] 61. spend the night on a house boat
- [ ] 62. watch a meteor shower from sea
- [ ] 63. dispose of a piece of trash that is not yours
- [ ] 64. complete the duval crawl
- [ ] 65. watch the conch shell drop on new year's eve
- [ ] 66. pick an avocado, make fresh guacamole, and plant the seed
- [ ] 67. ascend to the top of mount trashmore
- [ ] 68. leave your dollar at the no name pub
- [ ] 69. find an animal at the blue hole
- [ ] 70. snorkel christ of the abyss
- [ ] 71. make a list of things you love about the keys
- [ ] 72. leave a message in a bottle
- [ ] 73. join in the conch republic's bloody battle

- [ ] 74. lift a gold bar
- [ ] 75. find the best cuban mix on the island
- [ ] 76. sneak into a hotel hot tub
- [ ] 77. visit the statues of five oversized sea creatures
- [ ] 78. buy a plant from the marc house
- [ ] 79. search for sea glass
- [ ] 80. watch the bats come out at dusk
- [ ] 81. find the cashmier goats
- [ ] 82. nap in a hammock
- [ ] 83. befriend and name a key west chicken
- [ ] 84. learn to identify key west's architectural styles
- [ ] 85. visit robert the doll... if you dare
- [ ] 86. spend a day doing nothing
- [ ] 87. nurse a hangover in the sunshine
- [ ] 88. get a tattoo
- [ ] 89. wear a t-shirt with a silly saying around town
- [ ] 90. push your taste buds to the limit with a hot sauce tasting
- [ ] 91. snap your photo at mile marker zero
- [ ] 92. talk with a homeless person and learn their story
- [ ] 93. invent your own tropical drink
- [ ] 94. volunteer at a charity event
- [ ] 95. spot a water spout
- [ ] 96. dangle your legs off the old bahia honda bridge
- [ ] 97. win a game of 801 bingo
- [ ] 98. explore a side road in the middle keys
- [ ] 99. enter the hemingway look-alike contest, no matter who you look like
- [ ] 100. have a drink with the author of this book

add to the list

- [ ] 101.
- [ ] 102.
- [ ] 103.
- [ ] 104.
- [ ] 105.
- [ ] 106.
- [ ] 107.
- [ ] 108.
- [ ] 109.
- [ ] 110.
- [ ] 111.
- [ ] 112.
- [ ] 113.
- [ ] 114.
- [ ] 115.

notes

fat red pen

"Be proud of your accomplishments. They shape you." These words of wisdom came from an early mentor in my hotel career. Her appearance was impeccable, and although her outfits would change, the one part of her wardrobe that was always present was a fat red pen. Sometimes she clipped it to her blouse, or to the hem of her skirt, but it was always present. She would use it to sign her name in broad red strokes, so that even when she was not around, we were reminded of her presence. The fat red pen became a sign of power, of confidence, of accomplishment. All of us wanted a fat red pen, and she knew it.

Those words of wisdom came when I left hotels for cruise ships. "Be proud of your accomplishments. They shape you." As she said them, she produced a fat red pen and stuck it in my shirt pocket. It never became a regular part of my wardrobe, but the meaning behind the fat red pen has never left my side.

Maybe your book came with a fat red pen to check off your accomplishments. Maybe it didn't. No big deal. Any fat pen will do. The important thing is to be proud of your accomplishments and write with bold strokes wherever you go, be it checking off the things you did in this book or things you will do down the road. Be proud of your accomplishments. They shape you.

about the author

David L. Sloan discovered the Florida Keys in 1988 and has been a Key West resident since 1996. He is the founder of Key West's Original Ghost Tour, co-author of *Quit Your Job & Move to Key West* and author of nine titles, including *The Ultimate Key Lime Pie Cookbook*. A former satire columnist for the *Key West Citizen*, Sloan is also an avid food face artist, songwriter, and adventurer who likes to party.

Sloan has traveled through 50 states and more than 30 countries. He has been featured on The Travel Channel, History Channel, Biography Channel, Discovery Channel, Food Network, and BBC. He currently lives in Key West, Florida, with a blue attack vulture named TJ.

food face art

Bready La Head rolled out of bed and counted all of her blessings ~ not a care in the world ~ she was not a shy girl ~ and didn't care if the world saw her dressing!

Bready La Head

Food? Art? Both? View hundreds of Sloan's Food Faces and decide for yourself.

www.foodfaceart.com

PHANTOM**PRESS**
K E Y W E S T

Established Circa 1996

Ultimate Key Lime Pie Cookbook
Ghosts of Key West
Haunted Key West
Free Beer Tomorrow — The Paradise Columns
Quit Your Job & Move to Key West
Key West 101
The Key West Hangover Survival Guide
Don't Do It — 101 Reasons Not To Marry Her
He & She — A Wedding Story
Key West Cemetery Guide
Mandy Bolen's Tan Lines
Rob O'Neal's Photo Safari
Terry Schmida's True Crime Vol. I
Terry Schmida's True Crime Vol. II

www.phantompress.com

Interact with the author:
David L. Sloan
davidLsloan@mac.com
www.facebook.com/floridakeys
www.keylimecookbook.com
www.foodfaceart.com

"Life is either daring adventure or nothing. To keep our faces toward change and behave like free spirits in the presence of fate is strength undefeatable."

— **Helen Keller**

Made in the USA
Columbia, SC
10 January 2019